BOOK ANALYSIS

Written by Natacha Cerf
Translated by Rebecca Neal

AF143888

Essays

BY MICHEL DE MONTAIGNE

BOOK ANALYSIS

Bright Summaries.com

BOOK ANALYSIS

Fifty Shades of Grey Trilogy

BY E.L. JAMES

Shed new light
on your favorite books with

Bright
≣Summaries.com

www.brightsummaries.com

MICHEL DE MONTAIGNE 1

French writer and philosopher

ESSAYS 2

A life's work

SUMMARY 3

Book I
Book II
Book III

CONTEXT 26

Humanism
The composition and structure of the *Essays*

ANALYSIS 29

A self-portrait
Montaigne's writing
A critical judgement
Education
Religion
Human relationships
The search for wisdom

FURTHER REFLECTION 43

Some questions to think about...

FURTHER READING 45

MICHEL DE MONTAIGNE

FRENCH WRITER AND PHILOSOPHER

- **Born in Saint-Michel-de-Montaigne in 1533**
- **Died in 1592**
- **His work:**
    - The *Essays* (1590-1595)

Michel Eyquem de Montaigne (1533-1592) was a French writer, philosopher and politician during the Renaissance. He was involved in the political life of his country, notably as a counsellor of the Court of Aids in Périgueux and above all as mayor of Bordeaux. However, his main aspiration was to read and write, and this led him to embark on the writing of the *Essays*, a landmark of French literature which brings together his experiences, thoughts and reflections on the world.

Montaigne was a humanist who was primarily searching for wisdom beyond moral, political and religious beliefs.

ESSAYS

A LIFE'S WORK

- **Genre:** essay
- **Reference edition:** De Montaigne, M. (1965) *Essays*. Trans. Frame, D. Stanford: Stanford University Press.
- **First edition:** 1580
- **Themes:** introspection, the human condition, wisdom, friendship, education

The *Essays*, which first appeared in 1580, are Montaigne's main work: he began writing them in 1570. In them, the philosopher deals with many subjects, including medicine, knowledge and manners, which he combines with reflections on himself and on mankind in general.

The aim of his introspection is to discover the reality of the human condition: in order to grasp what man is, he observes, both in himself and in others, all the elements of life, no matter how lowly, ordinary or trivial.

SUMMARY

BOOK I

Chapter 1 – By diverse means we arrive at the same end

The behaviours and reactions of men vary. As such, it is difficult to know how to pacify someone we have offended.

Chapter 2 – Of sadness

Sadness is expressed in different ways. As a strong emotion, it overwhelms and crushes the soul.

Chapter 3 – Our feelings reach out beyond us

People should follow the advice of Socrates (Greek philosopher, 470-399 BC) and try to know themselves in the present. Instead, they always project themselves beyond the present out of fear, desire or hope.

Chapter 4 – How the soul discharges its passions on false objects when the true are wanting

People feel the need to express their emotions even when they cannot grasp the cause of this emotion. They will use any pretext and listener to find emotional relief.

Chapter 5 – Whether the governor of a besieged place should go out to parley

A worthy victory can only be won by courage and loyalty. Montaigne wonders whether the leader of a stronghold threatened by attackers should go out to negotiate, as the enemy offers, with the risk that this offer may be a trick to make him leave his post. Montaigne would trust the enemy.

Chapter 6 – Parley time is dangerous

How can one trust the enemy during negotiations? In any case, it is essential to remain loyal in all circumstances and not kill the enemy when they are advancing to sign the peace treaty.

Chapter 7 – That intention is judge of our actions

We must not judge actions, which people are not always in control of because they also depend on outside circumstances, but rather consider the intention.

Chapter 8 – Of idleness

When a person abandons public service in favour of study, they must rely on the discipline of writing; if not, the mind will spread out excessively.

Chapter 9 – Of liars

Liars have good memories because they must remember all their lies so as not to give themselves away. Montaigne has a bad memory. Lying is a perversion of the communication between men.

Chapter 10 – Of prompt or slow speech

Is it better to speak in a premeditated way like preachers, or spontaneously like orators? It can be beneficial to be spontaneous.

Chapter 11 – Of prognostications

It is strange and a pity that men are more attached to predictions than to living in the present.

Chapter 12 – Of constancy

Being constant means tolerating evils that cannot be avoided.

Chapter 13 – Ceremony of interviews between kings

Each country and each town has its own particular ceremonies. Montaigne recommends behaving well towards others by respecting their rules of politeness, as this is a way of making them well disposed towards you. However, excessive civility can lead to tipping over into impoliteness.

Chapter 14 – That the taste of good and evil depends in large part on the opinion we have of them

There is no absolute definition of evil: it varies from person to person, as some see it in poverty and others in suffering. As for happiness, the only people who are happy are those who are convinced that they are happy.

Chapter 15 – One is punished for defending a place obstinately without reason

One must not obstinately defend a stronghold against an excessively large number of enemies. In such a case, the virtue of courage would become a vice.

Chapter 16 – Of the punishment of cowardice

Cowards are already punished by shame. This is why they receive a greater degree of indulgence than those who are malicious.

Chapter 17 – A trait of certain ambassadors

Ambassadors are not content to merely report what they have seen or heard, but always add something in order to increase their own status.

Chapter 18 – Of fear

There are two ways of reacting to fear: being paralysed or behaving senselessly.

Chapter 19 – That our happiness must not be judged until after our death

Death is a moment of truth: because human affairs are so inconsistent and varied, a person only can know whether they have been happy or not on the last day of their life. Likewise, we cannot judge others until the moment of their end because it is only at the last second that appearances fall away and the truth comes out.

Chapter 20 – That to philosophize is to learn to die

Life is not measured by its length but by what we do with it: it is preferable to philosophise than to seek pleasure.

Chapter 21 – Of the power of the imagination

Belief in miracles and visions comes from the imagination.

The imagination even has the power to cure the body through remedies in which the sufferer believes.

Chapter 22 – One man's profit is another man's harm

This is not something we should criticise people for. It can be noted in the law of gain, by which the doctor enriches himself through the illnesses of his patients.

Chapter 23 – Of custom, and not easily changing an accepted law

Montaigne laments the fact that our habits are sometimes so deeply ingrained in us that they work against our basic nature and our spontaneity. The strength of habit can be seen in the variety of traditions and customs across the world: they are seen as laws.

Chapter 24 – Various outcomes of the same plan

The philosopher observes that the same intention lead to different actions. The reason that the consequences of an identical intention vary so much is that events are guided by chance.

Chapter 25 – Of pedantry

The pedant admires scholars so much that he does not think for himself and gives himself up completely to them. However, being wise means having a moral and critical mind.

Chapter 26 – Of the education of children

It is preferable for a child to be educated by someone with a well-formed mind rather than a head full of facts in order to learn to think morally and critically. The child must learn to observe, to listen and to put judgements and values into perspective. The most important thing is to make the child want to learn.

Chapter 27 – It is folly to measure the true and false by our own capacity

Credulity is ignorance but incredulity is arrogance: our power of judgement is not the reference of what is true and false, only God is.

Chapter 28 – Of friendship

Montaigne talks of his meeting with La Boétie (French writer, 1530-1563). Unlike family or romantic relationships, friendship is a perfect communication between two people who have freely chosen one another. The two friends knew each other completely, and when Étienne de la Boétie died a part of Montaigne went with him.

Chapter 29 – Twenty-nine sonnets of Etienne de La Boétie

This chapter no longer exists. Montaigne had initially placed his friend's sonnets here.

Chapter 30 – Of moderation

Moderation is essential. We must be careful: a virtue practised to excess becomes a vice.

Chapter 31 – Of cannibals

The philosopher demonstrates the relativity of value judgements: we are shocked by the cannibalism of the Brazilians, but they would be shocked by the unequal condition of men in Europe. We must not be so quick and so categorical in our rejection of things which are not in keeping with our own customs.

Chapter 32 – We should meddle soberly with judging divine ordinances

Nobody can predict God's plans, apart from imposters who take advantage of the credulity and ignorance of the people.

Chapter 33 – To flee from sensual pleasures at the price of life

Saint Hilary (315-367), Bishop of Poitiers, wanted his daughter to die while she was well-mannered, beautiful and rich; in short, destined for a happy future. He wanted to make her lose the taste for earthly pleasures so that she could be entirely joined with God.

Chapter 34 – Fortune is often met in the path of reason

Sometimes chance is more effective than reason.

Chapter 35 – Of a lack in our administrations

A flaw in our society is the fact that there is no place

where people could record their request for a worker. For example: I want to sell this, I need a carpenter, I am looking for someone to come with me to Rome, etc. In this way, everyone could announce their need and have it fulfilled.

Chapter 36 – Of the custom of wearing clothes

Clothes are a further proof of the power of custom because they exist even though they are not demanded by nature and sometimes do not even protect the wearer from cold or indecency.

Chapter 37 – Of Cato the Younger

Montaigne wants to pay tribute to Cato (Roman statesman and writer, 234-149 BC), who he thinks is unfairly denigrated. He depicts mankind's tendency to make hasty judgements, to reject difference, to be intolerant and to compare themselves to one another. Conversely, the philosopher is able to respect and praise people other than himself.

Chapter 38 – How we laugh and cry for the same thing

A victor can be happy for themselves and cry for the person they have defeated, in the same way that an avenger can be happy about this but also be sad at having caused pain through their vengeance.

Chapter 39 – Of solitude

True freedom is found in solitude, and we must be able to endure it. Being content with oneself is a positive thing.

Chapter 40 – A consideration upon Cicero

The vanity of this overly eloquent Roman orator (106-43 BC) is lamentable. He worked harder at making his speeches known than at standing out through his actions.

Chapter 41 – Of not communicating one's glory

Successful people like to communicate "their" glory, which was often won for them by others working without recognition.

Chapter 42 – Of the inequality that is between us

Only wisdom allows us to distinguish people from each other based on their quality. A king is no wiser or happier or more privileged than an ordinary person. The attributes of great figures are often imagined.

Chapter 43 – Of sumptuary laws

Royal orders against luxury from the 13th to the 16th centuries which governed the clothes a person could wear depending on their social rank only served to inspire envy towards the privileged, when in reality they should be scorned for only being able to distinguish themselves through luxury.

Chapter 44 – Of sleep

Sleep is important and is not in conflict with courage.

Chapter 45 – Of the battle of Dreux

Montaigne thinks that sacrificing some troops to win the overall battle can be a good military tactic.

Chapter 46 – Of names

People are wrong to grant so much importance to names because their identity does not result from them.

Chapter 47 – Of the uncertainty of our judgement

A decision may have different consequences than it was originally intended to. For example, lavishly arming soldiers with the aim of rousing their courage could on the contrary have the effect of distracting them from the combat as they are too busy admiring themselves. As such, the decisions taken and their outcomes, like events, depend above all on chance.

Chapter 48 – Of war horses

This is a chapter on the importance of horses throughout history.

Chapter 49 – Of ancient customs

People judge each other based on their customs even though these are all relative, as is proved by the changes in fashions and tastes in all subjects.

Chapter 50 – Of Democritus and Heraclitus

The human condition affected the Greek philosopher Heraclitus (circa 550-480 BC), while the philosopher Democritus (circa 460-370 BC) did not care about it and thought it was deserved. Montaigne thinks it is good to look into all ideas.

Chapter 51 – Of the vanity of words

Montaigne accuses rhetoric of being an art of speaking emphatically, without this emphasis translating into actions.

Chapter 52 – Of the parsimony of the ancients

Great men like Cato and Scipio Aemilianus, a Roman general who destroyed Carthage in the 2nd century BC, lived extremely frugally.

Chapter 53 – Of a saying of Caesar's

The Roman emperor Julius Caesar (100-44 BC) was just as surprised as Montaigne that the human mind dedicates itself to finding out the things that escape it rather than to understanding simple things.

Chapter 54 – Of vain subtleties

It is better to carry out effective actions than to search for complexity or rarity, or to practise the art of rhetoric.

Chapter 55 – Of smells

Smells have an impact on our mood, which should interest medicine or religion.

Chapter 56 – Of prayers

Prayer establishes a relationship between man and God, and rather than treating it as a magic spell, man should use it as a way of expressing to God his sincere pain at having offended him through his sins.

Chapter 57 – Of age

Instead of talking about old age, we should rather let young people act freely, because great actions are generally undertaken before the age of thirty.

BOOK II

Chapter 1 – Of the inconsistency of our actions

It is difficult to judge people because they always act inconsistently: their actions vary depending on the time and circumstances.

Chapter 2 – Of drunkenness

It destroys the body and the mind.

Chapter 3 – A custom of the island of Cea

Montaigne discusses suicide. Is it understandable, or can only God decide the moment of death? The philosopher thinks it can be courageous and justified in certain circumstances.

Chapter 4 – Let business wait till tomorrow

We must not be slaves to business, but be able to postpone it in order to feel free.

Chapter 5 – Of conscience

This chapter examines torture. The clear moral conscience of the innocent person is supposed to make them resistant to torture, but in reality it makes them admit anything, whereas the guilty person knows that if they resist the pain of torture they are saving themselves from a certain death.

Chapter 6 – Of practice

How can we practise for death? Sleep and fainting are similar experiences. But in order to learn to live and die, we must above all learn to know ourselves, and this is done through writing.

Chapter 7 – Of honorary awards

So that they remain an honour, awards should be given out sparingly according to true merit.

Chapter 8 – Of the affection of fathers for their children

The value, intelligence and morality of our children are not so much ours as theirs; this is why it is more right to love the products of our own minds, such as poetry, than our children.

Chapter 9 – Of the arms of the Parthians

This people from ancient Iran relied more on courage than on weapons when they fought. Now, men do not even have enough courage to take up weapons.

Chapter 10 – Of books

Montaigne reads for pleasure and to know himself better. He describes his favourite genres and authors, for example Virgil (1st century BC), Lucretius (98-55 BC), Catullus (1st century BC) and Horace (65-8 BC) for poetry.

Chapter 11 – Of cruelty

For Montaigne, morality is an innate virtue and a sensitivity which makes him automatically hate torture and hunting, two very cruel actions.

Chapter 12 – Apology for Raymond Sebond

This Spanish theologian (died in 1436) wanted to use reason to demonstrate the truth of religion. Montaigne refutes his argument because he views human reason as insufficient: all the schools in the world have not managed to discover the truth, which can only be revealed with the help of chance or God. Human reason is weak and must be made up for by the grace of faith.

Chapter 13 – Of judging the death of others

How can we evaluate the courage of the dying person when they are not aware that they are dying because their soul is just as weakened as their body?

Chapter 14 – How our mind hinders itself

A person who is undecided between two equivalent possibilities must nonetheless make a decision. Is this decision based on the irrational?

Chapter 15 – That our desire is increased by difficulty

Difficulty increases desire. This is also the case for life: its value comes from the prospect of death.

Chapter 16 – Of glory

Having lived calmly is the only honour there is. The other honours depend only on chance or on the approval of ignorant people who cannot see past appearances.

Chapter 17 – Of presumption

A presumptuous person prefers themselves to others. Montaigne has something of a tendency to overestimate other people. While he takes himself as an object of study, he belittles himself more than anything: he does not like his appearance, finds many flaws in himself, bows down before the ancients, etc. He does not expect any glory from his book.

Chapter 18 – Of giving the lie

Montaigne is not seeking posterity; he has written his book for himself (in order to make himself better through writing) and for those close to him.

Chapter 19 – Of freedom of conscience

This chapter discusses the religious freedom of conscience which was continually demanded by Protestants in the 16th century. Montaigne thinks that it stirs up civil dissent and spreads and increases disagreement. Furthermore, granting freedom of conscience weakens the religion concerned because difficulty rekindles faith, whereas ease dulls it.

Chapter 20 – We taste nothing pure

Suffering is always mixed with pleasure and, in laws, justice is always mixed with injustice. This composite material is within humankind and everywhere else.

Chapter 21 – Against do-nothingness

This is incompatible with the duties of emperors and of all people.

Chapter 22 – Of riding post

Montaigne traces the history of the means used by the princes of Antiquity to send their messages.

Chapter 23 – Of evil means employed to a good end

Because human beings are weak, they must use evil means to reach good ends. This is the case when the evils of war turn citizens away from idleness and scheming.

Chapter 24 – Of the greatness of Rome

Montaigne's contemporaries should have followed the custom of the Romans which involved leaving defeated kings their kingdoms.

Chapter 25 – Not to counterfeit being sick

Through pretending to be ill to get out of one task or another, a person becomes genuinely ill.

Chapter 26 – Of thumbs

Many customs demonstrate the importance of thumbs. One example among many is the Roman public giving a thumbs up or a thumbs down to decide the fate of gladiators in the amphitheatre.

Chapter 27 – Cowardice, mother of cruelty

Cowardice goes hand in hand with bloodthirstiness. Montaigne condemns the duels with took place during his time, often because of a mere peccadillo. The duel puts not only the duellers, but also their witnesses in danger. These combats are not carried out in the name of the public good, but in the name of self-interest. The blood spilled risks causing a haemorrhage of revenge. Tyrants and judges are also often cowardly; this is why they make death last and inflict torture.

Chapter 28 – All things have their season

There is a time for everything and therefore for every age: youth is for learning, and old age is for ridding oneself of one's possessions.

Chapter 29 – Of virtue

People must be judged over time because virtue can be due to chance or to an exceptional surge of the soul.

Chapter 30 – Of a monstrous child

The malformed person is said to be monstrous, but the divine decision responsible for this eludes humankind.

Chapter 31 – Of anger

Anger causes unjust punishments because it carries a person's soul away from them and guides their hand.

Chapter 32 – Defence of Seneca and Plutarch

Montaigne defends, among other texts, the stories of Plutarch (ancient Roman historian and thinker, c. 50-125), which were judged implausible by his peers.

Chapter 33 – The story of Spurina

Spurina disfigured himself out of fear of succumbing to the desires that his beauty aroused in others. He showed an excess of virtue, but showing moderation is a higher virtue than the excess of virtue.

Chapter 34 – Observations on Julius Caesar's methods of making war

The Roman emperor is an example: he demanded only bravery from his soldiers and punished only disobedience.

Chapter 35 – Of three good women

The philosopher gives three examples of exceptional women who, instead of mourning their husbands, joined them in death.

Chapter 36 – Of the most outstanding men

Homer (8th century BC), author of the *Iliad* and the *Odyssey*, is the first poet. Alexander the Great (356-323 BC), King of Macedonia, became the master of the world in his short life. Epaminondas (418-362 BC), Theban general and statesman, was a man of exemplary morals. These are three exceptional men.

Chapter 37 – Of the resemblance of children to fathers

Montaigne has inherited his father's illness: kidney stones. He therefore talks about doctors who contradict each other, and decides to leave himself in the hands of nature instead.

BOOK III

Chapter 1 – Of the useful and the honourable

Montaigne prefers not to be involved in public service, because in order to be politically effective this kind of business requires betrayal, lies and massacre.

Chapter 2 – Of repentance

Nobody knows a person as well as the person themselves. Consequently, each person's conscience is the only one capable of recognising their faults. The only thing is that we cannot repent of vices that are too deeply ingrained in us for us to be able to identify them as vices.

Chapter 3 – Of three kinds of association

The thinker likes to be with honest and virtuous men, with attractive women in a faithful romantic relationship, and finally with books. Of these three types of relationship, only the last one does not depend on someone else or on chance. Books are a refuge and a remedy for the sufferings of existence.

Chapter 4 – Of diversion

Is it preferable to console an afflicted heart by pitying it or by distracting it from its sadness? Montaigne finds that the human mind, which is unstable by nature, is easy to divert. The second method is therefore effective.

Chapter 5 – On some verses of Virgil

Montaigne draws on his memories of love to divert him from the sadness caused by the old age which is taking over him. He thinks that often marriage is not a choice, but an act of obedience to custom, and he speaks of sexuality which, although natural, is avoided in conversations between men. The thinker rejects jealousy in romantic relationships. Finally, according to him it is good to show patience in love: women are right to let themselves be courted for a long time. The philosopher uses the ancient poet Virgil (1st century BC) to support his idea that the allusive poetic style which awakens the imagination is entirely suitable for love.

Chapter 6 – Of coaches

Here Montaigne mentions means of transport. Some Roman emperors travelled in sumptuous horse-drawn carriages: so much luxury, when it is not deployed with the aim of embellishing or defending the kingdom, offends the people. A country's wealth does not belong to its head of state: the latter must simply administer the wealth for the good of the people. On the American continent there are kings who, as well as being courageous, are models of devotion to their subjects. Colonisation is therefore to be lamented because not only has it exterminated indigenous populations, but it has also denied Native American civilisation when there is less cruelty there than in Europe.

Chapter 7 – Of the disadvantage of greatness

It is certainly preferable to live an ordinary life than to be king, because how can a king demonstrate moderation when his power is absolute? Furthermore, he must often endure the hypocrisy of his subjects.

Chapter 8 – Of the art of discussion

Conversation between two equals who both listen to one another is stimulating for the mind. However, it is necessary to have an adversary who is on your level and to seek to reach the truth rather than to be right. Princes therefore cannot practise conversation because they have no equals and cannot reveal themselves to be weak or ignorant in certain subjects. Montaigne also likes to converse through reading, by trying to find the man behind the author.

Chapter 9 – Of vanity

Men like to travel to escape their day-to-day lives. As such, when he is travelling and is far away from public and private affairs, the author can think only of himself. It is a real pleasure to continually discover new things and to immerse himself in unfamiliar customs which he must try to understand. Finally, leaving his wife for a time is not a bad thing because absence makes the heart grow fonder.

Chapter 10 – Of husbanding your will

Montaigne thinks that a person should prefer themselves

over their duties to others; this is why he favours meditation over political and social commitments. He has taken up his position as mayor of Bordeaux, but not at the cost of his private life. Public affairs should only occupy a man in moderation because in any case the only judgement that counts is that of his own conscience, not that of others. He must therefore lend himself to others, but mostly be devoted to himself.

Chapter 11 – Of cripples

The crippled were ascribed unusual sexual skills. This is only true in the imagination, and the imagination influences the senses. It is therefore necessary to resist preconceived opinions and avoid judging, because only God can judge. Similarly, Montaigne is against putting witches to death, as they are the victims of unfounded prejudices.

Chapter 12 – Of physiognomy

Rather than thinking for themselves, people follow collective opinions and rumours. They are also inclined to prefer artifice and the possession of things they do not have, whereas they should follow nature, which is calming. Peasants who live in harmony with nature have more courage than men who have been taught by science: they calmly face plague and death. Indeed, nature helps people to prepare for death by reminding them that it is no use thinking about it endlessly, because that is the order of things. It is better to live according to the laws of nature than to aspire to perfection.

Physiognomy does not always go hand in hand with the inner being, as evidenced by the ugliness of the Greek philosopher Socrates (470-399 BC).

Chapter 13 – Of experience

Letting oneself by guided by experience is the best way of discovering the truth. This is also the case in the exercise of introspection: a person must observe themselves from day to day in order to know themselves. Montaigne once again recommends following nature, which dictates better than doctors what is beneficial and fulfilling for us. He finishes his work with an ode to life, to self-mastery and to moderation, which are the virtues of the truly wise man.

CONTEXT

Montaigne was a Renaissance humanist. Humanism is an intellectual movement which originated in Italy in the 14th century, before reaching the rest of Europe in the 15th and 16th centuries. It spread thanks to advances in printing and the exodus of many Greek scholars who took refuge in Italy after the city of Constantinople was conquered by the Turks.

The presence of these Greek scholars in Italy made humanists want to obtain ancient texts in their original language and not their Latin translations, which were annotated with a whole series of glosses and commentaries, in order to be able to understand and interpret the message of the ancients for themselves. This return to ancient sources and the emphasis on critical thinking are two of the main characteristics of humanism. Men of letters at this time also wanted, in the same spirit, to read the Bible for themselves without any intermediary.

Associated with this undertaking was the idea that the study of literature makes man more worthy. It was therefore a matter of perfecting oneself as a human being and at the same time being amazed at the greatness of certain men, notably ancient authors and figures such as Socrates. The ancient world is full of examples of heroism, whereas at the time when Montaigne was alive this was no longer the case. The philosopher was greatly attracted by the liberty, justice and prosperity of the Roman republic.

Humanists, who wanted to get as close as possible to their models, granted major importance to education, which can make man better: one is not born, but rather becomes, a man. This takes place through a great appetite for knowledge fed by cosmopolitanism. In this way, education occurs by experiencing the world.

THE COMPOSITION AND STRUCTURE OF THE *ESSAYS*

The *Essays* are spread across three books. In this work, Montaigne's aim is to get to know himself better by exercising his judgement on several subjects. The unstructured succession of these very varied subjects means that the book is nothing like an ordered overview.

Books I and II were published simultaneously in 1580. The first comprises philosophical reflections on death, friendship, education and solitude, as well as some historical or military observations, while the second is more focused on the author: he talks about his taste in literature, his aim of depicting himself and his viewpoint on topics such as suicide, parent-child relationships, cruelty and illness.

Book III appeared in 1588 and focuses on political and philosophical reflections: individual conscience and daily experience give access to the truth. Montaigne reveals his philosophy, which is to follow nature.

The main themes of the *Essays* are as follows:

• Critical thinking;

- The condemnation of all forms of violence (hunting, war, torture, etc.);
- Education and travel: the goal is not to accumulate knowledge, but to hone one's judgement;
- Openness to others: Montaigne is interested in everyone, from distant tribes to those close to him (love, friendship, conversation);
- The body and illness: as somebody who was ill himself, Montaigne knew suffering and the way that the mind influences the body. He makes health the highest good;
- Old age and death. The philosopher wanted to fight against death, but he ends up accepting it as an essential part of life;
- Philosophy, morality and religion. Experience is preferable to abstract thoughts.

The essay is a literary genre created by Montaigne. His aim is to exercise his judgement, which draws questions that need answering from various subjects, but this takes place without the deduction of certainties. In other words, it is a personal commentary on one or several chosen themes. Although the "I" takes centre stage, the essay is not an autobiography since it falls under the category of knowledge and not a life story.

ANALYSIS

The aim of Montaigne's work is self-knowledge. The author depicts himself without artifice and in a natural way so that after his death his loved ones can find him there as they knew him. He draws a physical, moral and intellectual portrait of himself, but physical description takes on less importance than the compilation of his experiences, of the books he has read, and of his meetings with men.

Montaigne's goal is certainly not to glorify himself, defend himself or portray himself as a moraliser, but he recognises the proud aspect of his undertaking: he is necessarily often the only character presented and, when he is not describing his activities and what has happened to him, he is expressing his opinions and his own sensitivity. However, for all that he does not feel indulgence when he looks at himself. Indeed, Montaigne does not hesitate to criticise himself and inform the reader of his flaws. Furthermore, he says nothing of the honours and rewards that he has received during his life, of the humanitarian actions he has carried out, or even of the evidence of affection and trust he has received. The author is looking to live at peace with himself rather than to glorify himself.

In short, writing is a means of getting to know oneself, and Montaigne is only aiming to discover himself. However, this attempt goes beyond biography because it also intends to depict man in general: the philosopher considers himself a sample of humanity. This knowledge of the human condition takes place through the description of human actions as a whole and of the traditions, customs, words and claims of men. It is in the detail of the everyday rather than in great achievements that we can know all about human beings.

This undertaking had many effects on the author: it helped him to better understand others, to reflect on the religious, political and social problems of his time, to stabilise himself, and to shape his personality.

MONTAIGNE'S WRITING

The writing of the *Essays* tests out the fluctuations of reflection and the twists and turns of an open mind, which conveys the diversity of the world and of humankind and allows us to gain a new perspective on things.

Montaigne's writing is characterised by its simplicity. The philosopher's project excludes any rhetoric: the language must be naïve and natural in order to remain close to the "I" and not disfigure thoughts by decoration. It is not an exercise in style but an exercise in reflection. However, the choice of words is nonetheless important in the translation of ideas. As such, the style serves the thought and not the other way round. Likewise, Montaigne adapts the rhythm of sentences to his content, using a natural form of expression if the idea he wants to convey is simple, an incisive writing style if he is trying to, for example, to imitate Seneca, and long passages with parenthetical elements if he is trying to express the twists and turns of a train of thought.

However, the philosopher does resort to some stylistic devices which allow him to add nuance to his remarks:

- Antithesis, which involves bringing together two opposing ideas in the same statement with the aim of emphasising the contrast between them: "For we move other weapons, this one moves us; our hand does not guide it, it guides our hand; it holds us, we do not hold it" (Book II, Chapter 31).
- Comparisons and metaphors. Comparisons establish a relationship of analogy between two ideas or two objects: "Vice leaves repentance in the soul, like an ulcer in the flesh" (Book III, Chapter 2). Metaphor differs from comparison in that it has no comparative word, but refers to an object or an idea using a word which is suited to another object or another idea: "the heart and life of a great and triumphant emperor is the breakfast of a little worm" (Book II, Chapter 12).
- Irony, which involves saying the opposite of what you really think. In Chapter 6 of Book III Montaigne makes ironic remarks about the supposed superiority of Europeans over Indians.

Finally, since the philosopher's aim is not to persuade but to make his reader think, he uses:

- Examples, anecdotes and observations which contradict or support certain ideas;
- Recurrence. Several of the subjects dealt with are recurrent and appear in different chapters. For example, Montaigne can develop a topic from the point of view of

justice, then later from the point of view of morality;

- Appeals. Among others, he appeals against Raymond Sebond and in favour of cannibals.

A CRITICAL JUDGEMENT

Montaigne has often been considered to be fearful of change and innovation, but in reality he often criticised the established order:

- The demystification of great men. This involves distinguishing the function of the prince from man as he is, because great men are not beings who are made up differently from other men and can very well be mediocre. Moreover, often these lofty men who should display the virtues of humanity, truth, loyalty, temperance and justice do not do so, and that is deplorable. Instead of seeking to win the love of the people, they want to make themselves more attractive through luxury or impose themselves through fear. They are cowardly and cruelly exterminate their opponents rather than facing up to them. Montaigne thinks that these bloodthirsty princes should follow the example of the kings of Peru and Mexico, who are courageous and loved by their people.
- Criticism of the law. The law results from arbitrary decisions made by weak and vain men; this is why it fluctuates depending on the time period and the customs of countries when it should be unchanging and based on reason. Furthermore, Montaigne considers it a shame that laws are written in a language which is obscure and unintelligible to the people, who therefore cannot

understand them or respect them. Additionally, this language problem gives rise to different interpretations which are often contradictory. The philosopher also rebukes laws inherited from Roman law for no longer being suitable for the time and for often being unjust (such as torture), and laments the fact that law is often priceless and therefore not accessible to everybody.

- Denunciation of war. Montaigne thinks that war has no other aim than to kill, which proves our stupidity and imperfection. Although it could be evidence of bravery among the ancients, during his time it was nothing but cruelty and petty ambitions. Waging a war means abandoning individual morality.
- Anticolonialism. The Spanish and Portuguese conquerors engaged in appalling massacres. Vain and greedy, they allowed themselves a wholly brutal absolute power, going so far as to deny the humanity of the Native Americans. Colonisation unfolded in unspeakable cruelty: towns were razed to the ground, nations were exterminated, and people were betrayed, threatened and destroyed. In view of this, Montaigne asks himself: of the Europeans and the indigenous peoples, who is really barbaric and savage?

As we have said above, Montaigne was nonetheless not in favour of innovation and was wary of reforms, which he saw as dangerous. Indeed, in his view the possibility of social life is based on obedience to the established order. However, for all that he is not conservative, and he does still distinguish between the public and the private: the individual must follow the laws of the princes outside and their own laws within themselves. Within themselves, therefore, people benefit from complete freedom to think and to criticise anything that they judge unjust.

EDUCATION

The philosopher formulates pedagogical principles based on the humanists' common belief that man is naturally good: inclination towards evil comes from a bad education or from company which pushes him into sin and malice. Children must therefore be kept away from these harmful influences so that their good nature can be preserved.

Montaigne is opposed to the collective education given out in schools because he sees it as incapable of shaping different minds. Rather, he recommends an individual education given by a private tutor who is attentive to the child's nature. In addition, dialogue should be favoured over teaching from the front of the classroom.

According to him, the key features of a good education are as follows:

- The exercise of critical thinking. The child must be confronted with various pieces of knowledge and varied viewpoints so as to be able to compare and critique them. This leads them to question some principles and adopt others. In short, Montaigne is against learning things by heart: according to him, a "well-made" head is better than a "well-filled" one.
- The exercise of the body. The body should be toughened so that it no longer fears cold or darkness. In this way, the

muscles are hardened and the child is trained to suffer less. In Montaigne's ideal education, the body is respected as much as the mind since the moral and physical faculties are linked. Testing the body leads to mastering the passions and the instincts.

- The development of an open mind. Learning is done less in books than in nature itself: it is necessary to learn to observe, reason and understand everything in order to then acquire a particular science which the well-formed mind chooses freely. This happens through spending time in the company of men and through conversing as much with peasants as with nobles; in short, through contact with all aspects of life.
- Travelling. This allows the child to face new and unknown things. Significantly, Montaigne takes an interest in other peoples, their customs and their lifestyles with the aim of understanding them, not judging them. He sees travelling as a way of enriching one's own knowledge, not as an attempt to assimilate the other to oneself. The student should adopt the same attitude in order to become tolerant.

The purpose of this education is moral. It should allow the pupil to become better and wiser, able to recognise and choose the truth.

RELIGION

Montaigne disagrees with the theologian Raymond Sebond, who emphasises the power of reason, because reason is a gift from God, in service of faith. Indeed, he considers human reason incapable of knowing God since man is entirely unlike him. According to the philosopher, it is sacrilege to think that God is anything like man: God is transcendent and should not in any way be mixed with our corruption and misery.

Likewise, it is a mistake to seek to penetrate his designs because they are opaque to us. Montaigne gives the example of the disabled: although others consider them to be imperfect, the fact that God's creations are supposed to be perfect perhaps means that these beings are not at all monstrous in the eyes of God. It is therefore not up to us to judge his works or his intentions.

Montaigne conceives God as transcendent, but not always intervening in human affairs. Consequently, it is foolish for men to address him with prayers filled with demands. Faith should not be based on events: God is not the cause of everything that happens to us and more often uses a kind of justice that is unknown to us than his power. As such, faith should only express man's recognition towards God, who allows him to push back the limits of his weak nature. In fact, human beings can only be raised through divine grace, and we must thank God for this in our prayers rather than addressing our desires to him.

Men can only be saved by the grace of God, not by their actions or their works. This idea is one of the challenges to Catholic dogma by the Protestant Reformation. Luther (German reformer, 1483-1546) translated the Bible into German with the aim of allowing everyone to read it and interpret it without having to go through the authority of the priest. This spirit of free enquiry with regard to the Scriptures led to the rejection of some other dogmas such as the worship of saints, and sacraments outside of baptism and Communion. As such, Protestantism is a pared-down religion which removes the intermediaries between man and God. However, Montaigne does not look favourably on the Protestant Reformation: he deems it ridiculous to meddle in these questions due to the weakness of the human mind. Furthermore, these steps are harmful to morality and social life. The conflict between Catholics and Protestants turns all too often into fanaticism: both sides should demonstrate moderation.

Moderation should be at the heart of all actions, and is the element which defines moral conduct. The philosopher emphasises this point more than the content of the belief, since individual judgement is too weak and inconsistent to speak about belief. Being moderate means being modest. Conversely, he criticises excessive piety which conceals hypocrisy, hatred, greed and injustice.

Montaigne also thinks that religion is a cultural legacy and a social phenomenon which thus experiences birth and decline. It is chance rather than an act of faith that makes a person obey one tradition or another, and it is education more than revelation that makes a man adopt one religion or another.

Although the author of the *Essays* is Catholic, he nonetheless distances himself from Catholicism on some points. For example:

- he barely talks about the Virgin, relics or miracles;
- he defends suicide, which was condemned by the Church;
- his belief in sins and repentance is limited;
- for him, paradise and earthly life after the Resurrection are absurd ideas.

This raises questions about Montaigne's faith. In reality, he follows a natural religion: he wavers between fideism, needing to base his relationship with God on a faith that is independent of reason, and agnosticism, denying that man is capable of rising to metaphysical concepts.

HUMAN RELATIONSHIPS

Montaigne enjoys life and the encounters it brings. Emotions and feelings have an important place in his life, and he seeks out the company of others. In particular, he refers to two kinds of relationship:

- Relationships with women. The philosopher is not ashamed to speak freely about sexuality, which he considers natural, necessary and just. For Montaigne, love is above all about pleasure and fervent desire. However, as the body and the mind are closely linked, the sexual act stimulates the mind. This is why he considers poetic language to be particularly suited to conveying love. Montaigne does not envisage intellectual friendship with women, subject to some exceptions. Nonetheless, he has no objections to letting his wife manage his land when he leaves to travel, which could be considered a form of equality. It is therefore difficult to define Montaigne's exact views on the roles and status of women: sometimes they are at the mercy of their bodies, capricious, childish and poorly suited to education; sometimes they are cut from the same cloth as men, equal but made different only by custom, and he finds it normal that they would rebel against the rules that men try to impose on them. Moreover, for him marriage is merely a necessary social deal which is made out of respect for customs, but which is incompatible with desire because it must be strict and pious. As such, there is always a distance between men and women.

- Friendship. In friendship, there is no distance. His relationship with Étienne de la Boétie is proof of this: it was exceptional and never weakened. The advantage of friendship over other kinds of relationship is that it is based on an equality which could be taken as a model for justice in society. It joins together two mature and equal men: Montaigne and La Boétie are two wills who freely chose one another. After the death of his friend, Montaigne only lives a half-life. This is why he throws himself into writing the *Essays*. In this way, La Boétie is at the centre of his life and of his work.

That said, although Montaigne appreciates relationships with others, he is no less critical towards social life. Indeed, he thinks that social life is teeming with ambition, lust and greed: if a man claims that he is turning towards the public good rather than his own personal interests, this is to extract greater personal gain from the public through social relationships. In this context, it is thus better to develop a taste for solitude, as at the centre of the crowd good people are hard to come by and bad people are contagious. If a person remains there, they either become like the others or too often hate other people. As such, the wise man flees the crowd so as not to have to tolerate its vices. Instead, he seeks a calmer and more comfortable way of living.

However, keeping away from people is not enough to destroy vice: changing one's location does not resolve the problem. Instead, the individual must work on themselves because we are only completely free when our heads are no longer full of the things we left behind and when we are freed from all worldly vices (ambitions of glory, desire for pleasure and wealth, etc.). Isolating the soul within itself leads to the true self-knowledge that Montaigne aspires to for himself and others. This is a matter of observing oneself clearly and not being influenced by the approval or censure of other people. This is why it is necessary to take models from Antiquity and allow them to control our intentions: the respect that we have for them will put us back on the right track.

THE SEARCH FOR WISDOM

Montaigne was influenced by the sceptic philosopher Pyrrho (365-275 BC). His readings lead him to the conclusion that man cannot reach the truth, particularly because his senses constantly deceive him. This is evidenced by the plurality and diversity of philosophical doctrines: man seems incapable of fixing the essence of humanity. He only has access to appearances, but these are distorted by his sensory perceptions. The experiment with the stick which appears diagonally when it is submerged in water proves the impossibility of trusting the senses. Montaigne also refers to the influence of the state of a person's health on their perception of things: they do not appear to us in the same way if a problem with our bodies is affecting our mood. Finally, the imagination plays a major part in incorrect perceptions of reality. As such, man must acknowledge that he is ignorant and unstable: he constantly goes from one state of mind to another and changes his ideas depending on the circumstances. Consequently, he must refrain from categorical judgements and become aware of the subjective and provisional nature of his opinions: these are the premises of reason.

According to Montaigne, being wise involves:

- Being moderate. Moderation and modesty are essential. A person must withdraw from worldly goods, limit their activities and master their passions. This is necessary so as to not suffer life's setbacks, to achieve inner calm and to preserve one's self-control.
- Being virtuous. This does not mean winning glory and enjoying a good reputation, because in these domains everything is based on appearances and delusions. The truly virtuous man exercises his wisdom alone and on a daily basis, seeking, like Socrates, to know himself.
- Trusting nature. When Montaigne started writing the *Essays*, his kidney stones were causing him a great deal of suffering and brought him close to death, but also allowed him to discover that pain, through contrast, lets the sufferer appreciate pleasure. He therefore decides to not put himself in the hands of doctors, but to let nature

do its work. He considers nature to be the best guide: man can only find happiness by being in harmony with himself here on earth, by continuing to be himself and by knowing how to recognise and savour the simple pleasures that are accessible to everyone; in short, by living according to his nature and according to nature as a whole. Nature does things well because it has made necessary actions like eating, sleeping, drinking and making love pleasant, and is at the root of all the most valuable goods.

FURTHER REFLECTION

SOME QUESTIONS TO THINK ABOUT...

- What links can you establish between Montaigne's point of view on education and that of Rabelais (c. 1494-1553) in *Pantagruel*? In what ways do the methods advocated by the two authors differ from the teaching methods of their time?
- In what ways does *Utopia* by Thomas More (1478-1535) agree with Montaigne's point of view on education?
- What does "being oneself" mean for Montaigne?
- What literary genre do the *Essays* belong to, essay or autobiography? Justify your answer.
- In what ways is this work humanist?
- Why is moderation so important for Montaigne?
- In what ways can it be said that Montaigne is a sceptic?
- In "Apology for Raymond Sebond", Montaigne criticises philosophers. Explain the reasons for this.
- What is Montaigne's religion? Do you know of any other authors/philosophers who share his point of view?
- Did the Wars of Religion have an impact on the *Essays*? Explain.
- What can we say about argumentation in the *Essays*?
- In what ways can a parallel by established between La Fontaine fable "The Two Friends" and the conception of friendship in Montaigne's work?

We want to hear from you!
Leave a comment on your online library
and share your favourite books on social media!

FURTHER READING

REFERENCE EDITION

- De Montaigne, M. (1965) *Essays*. Trans. Frame, D. Stanford: Stanford University Press.

REFERENCE STUDIES

- Bakewell, S. (2011) *How to Live: A Life of Montaigne in One Question and Twenty Attempts at an Answer*. London: Vintage.
- Boudou, B. (2001). *Essais. Michel de Montaigne*. Paris: Hatier.
- Holyoake, J. (1984) *Montaigne: "Essais" (Critical Guides to French Texts)*. London: Grant & Cutler Ltd.

Bright ≡Summaries.com

BOOK ANALYSIS

More guides to rediscover your love of literature

Animal Farm
BY GEORGE ORWELL

The Stranger
BY ALBERT CAMUS

Harry Potter and the Sorcerer's Stone
BY J.K. ROWLING

The Silence of the Sea
BY VERCORS

Antigone
BY JEAN ANOUILH

The Flowers of Evil
BY BAUDELAIRE

www.brightsummaries.com

© **BrightSummaries.com, 2016. All rights reserved.**

www.brightsummaries.com

Ebook EAN: 9782806288042

Paperback EAN: 9782806290823

Legal Deposit: D/2016/12603/838

Cover: © Primento

Digital conception by Primento, the digital partner of publishers.